A World Where Many Worlds Fit

Benjamin Dangl

Fomite
Burlington, VT

ISBN-13: 978-1-959984-00-9
Library of Congress Control Number: 2022952360

Fomite
58 Peru Street
Burlington, VT 05401
www.fomitepress.com
06-08-2023

Contents

Part V — Water Worlds: Seas of Possibility

Part VI — Homeward: The Road is a Hammock for Our Hearts

"In the world we want, everyone fits.
We want a world where many worlds fit."
— Subcomandante Marcos, Zapatistas

Preface

This book celebrates a world where many worlds fit. It reports from beyond the homogenizing forces of global capitalism, from decolonized street markets, scattered autonomous territories, and peoples' orchestras of the road. It records my attempts to distill what I saw in travels around the world while working as a journalist.

Awed by these streetscapes at dawn, these bus rides under Andean stars, these revolutions and defeats, I wanted to deepen my experience of them by writing it down. Bearing witness was a way of moving through the world, rendering a scene in words the way a camera shutter catches light.

The photography here is a part of that same process of seeing and gathering. The snapshots in these pages are organized to complement the words. They do not always depict the same location as the poems, but convey a similar feeling through visual poetry. (See photo locations listed at the end of the book.) Like the trains and taxis described throughout these pages, the words and photos are a means of transportation, providing windows through which to see.

As I created the writing and photography collected in this book over a twenty year period, I also worked as a journalist, reporting for social justice, following causes and movements, and investigating moments of inequality and liberation. This work resulted in three books and hundreds of articles published on Indigenous movements and politics in the Andes, working class struggles in the global south, leftist political victories in Latin America, US imperialism, women's rights, and environmental justice.

Following those stories took me to Amazonian rivers polluted by Cargill pesticides, rickshaw union efforts in India, and popular uprisings in Bolivia. As I conducted research and interviewed those affected for my nonfiction work, I also recorded the most compelling scenes from these travels in hundreds of personal notebooks. What you have here is a revised selection from those thousands of pages.

This book is a journey in which, following the spirit of the Zapatista saying, everything fits. The poems and photographs are organized in a way to conjure the experience of traveling through worlds of cities, streets, wildernesses, and waterways:

Part I: *Between Two Worlds: Departures and Arrivals* explores the vivid newness of seeing a country for the first time, the lights of the city from the descending plane, the night scenes along the train tracks. It reaches into the potent moments between leaving and landing, of arriving and knowing a new place: the engine of travel.

Part II: *The Organismal City: Urban Ecosystems* brings the reader into mountain city markets, the bowels and roaming dogs of urban spaces, a Havana New Year, an Andean carnival. Cities are concrete ecosystems containing many organismal worlds unto themselves, each with their own ways of breathing, moving, digesting.

The city gives way to Part III: *Streetscapes: Where the Waves Gather*, where revolutionaries organize their barricades, where fireworks ricochet in Delhi, and where bankers sing of Che Guevara while kids search for dinner in garbage cans. Worlds converge and celebrate in the street, where the private becomes public, where wanderers and workers, street vendors and outlaws, families and drunks gather, finding a common home and passage.

The bus follows the river to Part IV: *Riding Through the Wilderness: On the Edges of Maps*, on jungle roads past tuba players at dawn, coca farmers, weapon vendors and herds of camels, cumbia music echoing toward jagged mountain horizons. The bus window is the traveler's eternal companion, offering rolling views and fleeting insights into rural, roadside worlds.

The journey continues through Part V: *Water Worlds: Seas of Possibility*, where fishermen play the puppet strings of their nets, waterfalls catch on fire at night, bullet holes by the river tell of coups and uprisings, and funeral pyres light the shores of the Ganges. Bodies of water evoke the possibility of travel, their horizons and ports a reminder of the vastness of the world, their seas a metaphor for movement.

The book concludes with Part VI: *Homeward: The Road is a Hammock for Our Hearts*, where a lightning storm in mid-flight, Valentine's Day in Paraguay, and a tropical ferry ride embody the sweet weariness of finding home in the journey, across the invisible maps of a world of many worlds.

Part I
Between Two Worlds: Departures and Arrivals

Riding Seasickness Across the Invisible Map of Night

We ride our seasickness
across the border,
a bag of books
spilling onto the floor.

The city out the window
could be anywhere.

The only green in night's inverted constellation
is an empty soccer field,
glowing under the shock
of its many moons.

The strangest geography
is our plane
shooting over the earth
without permission,
clandestine in the nation
of the sky.

Its propeller heart
is never tired.

We are a flashlight
broadcasting into the void.

Only the darkness is bigger than us.

The plane rides the invisible map of night,
a bloodhound following its nose
to the next city.

This is the Jungle We Have All Been Waiting For

The bus station is a dark field of vacant seats.
This is the jungle we've all been waiting for.

There are no regressive lunchtime vistas.
All the passports have been stolen.

You can't eat from the fruit trees in paradise.
Someone else already owns them.

A bus driver blinks into the supernatural glow
of a billboard ad for a beachfront motel.

Travel is the place we are moving towards,
the picture of it in our minds before we get there.

Unheard Music Controls the Rhythmic Press

Lurching into motion,
passengers sing in their seats,
playing drums
past India's fields,
forests, rice paddies,
countless shacks with children waving smiles.

The train slides through the fields,
a mechanical snake
swaying back and forth,
steady as a ship,
but bound to the earth; metal against metal.

The rails thrash below
like the persistent throbbing
of a bass.

Outside the window,
towns curl into view;
a scattering in the distance of fields and huts.

On the train, people sleep on shoulders,
stare snugly against one another
into soda bottles, bags of chips, books.

It is a crowded, heaving mass,
moving and reacting in time to
an unheard music
controlled by the rhythmic press
of the train against the land.

Paraguayan Dawn

We wake up in the dark when the stars still hold up the sky.

I shuffle out to the road,
careful not to step on any snakes.

Roosters' crows fill the air,
dozens of them in a chorus,
no one with the same tone or style.
They respond to each other,
their frequencies bouncing back and forth
across the static of dawn.

Motorcycles come from the distance,
spilling zig zagging tubes of light into the dark.

Riding into town as the sun rises orange,
the palm trees black in silhouette.

Ducks huddle in a yard,
a cat crouching in red dirt,
the stars' brightness dulled by the sun.

The landscape softens,
house lights bounce past.

Arriving at a soccer field:
white gnats cloud the air
and roosters continue the morning's raw song.

Garbage Snowstorm

The rooster on the side of the road to Potosí
doesn't budge as the bus roars past,
windows rattling with cumbia music.

Propaganda from recent elections
fades on the mud walls of rural homes.

A snowstorm of garbage fills the air.

Through the colorful debris
families pick among trash,
and a sign welcomes us to the city.

Towering over its short buildings and church steeples
is Cerro Rico, or Rich Hill,
the source of the looted silver that powered Europe's capitalist empire.

Like the city that grew out of its riches,
the mountain is now a bruised pile
of what it once was.

As the bus rolls into town,
graffiti on a battered red wall announces,
"Here there is no president."

The Beach Has a New Car Smell

We drink beer as warm
as the inside of a tuba
while bus tickets grow out of the ground like weeds
and palm trees catch on fire at night
so the fish can see.

All the boats around here are guns
with sunglasses.

The only wildlife is on TV or being cooked over an open fire.

When the tide comes in,
nothing shows up but umbrellas and piano keys.

The beach has a new car smell.

The stomach of history returned our calls.

We are at home in this homesickness.

Part II
The Organismal City: Urban Ecosystems

Illegal Spring

Skyscrapers are all holding their breath
and the subways just inhale.

Sun pounds at the asphalt
until the heat and tar surrender
in a soft release
and mirages dance and rise
from the surface of the streets.

Ink is melting off the newspapers,
stoplights are drunk with humidity,
but the mosquitos buzz on,
spouting rumors
from their air-conditioned minds.

Evening arrives like a snowstorm
in the middle of a burning building:

People crawl from behind fans
and gather on street corners
as the sweat-soaked day
oozes self-consciously into night.

Even when there is no rain,
small streams run
between the tracks in the subway.

They are made of the slimy byproducts
of a city with too many things to buy.

The urban waste gathers
between those steel rails
and rots into the soggy pages
of world history.

These are the smells of the city's roots,
desperately reaching into the tired earth
with an unnatural hunger,
hiccupping out of drain pipes and sewers,
bubbling into the city streets –
a fifth season,
an illegal spring.

Rain in the Valley, Snow in the Mountains

La Paz is a city
with so many ways
of seeing itself,
an urban canyon
of new skyscrapers
and old churches.

Fist fights break out in the union office,
a dog licks frozen vomit off a sidewalk
on a cold Sunday morning,
teenagers deal drugs out of bullets shells,
an ex-vice president buys a newspaper,
a guy takes a dump in a glass-walled
ATM booth in broad daylight.

There's the furious dog
attacking the rear bumper of a taxi
for an entire block
next to trucks overflowing
with recently-arrived corn and potatoes,
watermelon piled high on the sidewalk
and sliced open,
while white buses fuse
into one honking traffic jam.

The sun burns away cold fog
as the song "Baa, Baa, Black Sheep" plays
over a congested intersection.

The sporadic rattle of firecrackers
throughout the night mixes with brass bands
whose sounds come in waves and then disappear
as the band moves on and rain thickens.

A thousand feet up, street markets
writhe with night activity,
light oozing out of storefronts
onto the traffic-clogged streets,
people sell coca leaves, masks, mining helmets,
calling out into the cold dark for customers.

La Paz is a city the morning after carnival
when some people are still drunk,
wandering home in the rain-soaked streets,
through puddles littered
with dog shit and busted balloons.

Here the open-air market smells
of cold mountains,
muddy water flows down drain gutters,
pedestrians hold hands and scold kids,
spider webs of electric lines weave
from building to building,
garbage is pounded into dirt roads
by constant traffic,
and buses compete for riders.

It all weaves together,
forms an equation,
a hive of urban bees
moving the seething city.

When it rains in the valley,
it snows in the mountains.

Broken Blender at the Dog Fight

Sunlight at dawn makes the old city look young.

A constellation of stains on the taxi's pink seat covers
tell a hundred tales.

One lone bus roars through an empty intersection.
Its bumper reads: "My blood is a river that carries your name."

A broken blender is on sale at El Alto's sprawling street market.

Drunken men stumble through puddles,
half-dancing to the morning's cumbia music.

Vendors unpack used clothes from the US,
boxes of candy, arming their day.

The rain pounds down,
drowning out all other noise
until the city disappears.

The mountains are bigger than the soccer stadium.
A white cloud over the sausage stand
mixes with red smoke bombs
set off for each goal.

A lone bag of peanuts sails hopefully through the air.

A car passes with furniture piled five feet high on its roof.
An older woman is in such a hurry to catch her bus
she forgets her sack of potatoes on the sidewalk.
It sits, lonely in a cloud of exhaust.

Dogs fight each other in the middle of the road.

A ham sandwich as big as a truck
poses on a billboard above the traffic.

The side of a passing bus promises: "Security, Elegance, Adventure."

Upside-Down Carnival

The streets of Oruro are clogged with people
whose bodies surge with alcohol
and the unceasing beats of marching brass bands.

Sweat pours from the faces of the carnival dancers
stomping through the city for hours.

Revelers spray aerosol cans of foam at each other,
toss water balloons,
chew dried llama meat,
snap photos.

The whole city moves with an exhausted
but determined energy,
buoyed by cans of warm beer.

Costumed dancers spin past
depicting a synthesis of heaven and hell,
where the world is tossed upside down
and miners become devils.

After carnival, when the fiesta's aftermath
has long been pressed
into the streets by the celebrating thousands,
the train to Uyuni sputters reluctantly out of the station.

Its musty cocoon rattles against cold tracks
past small towns where occasional streetlights bring into view
an alleyway soccer game,
couples stumbling out of bars.

The moon shines on plants clinging to dry farmland
rising up toward distant mountains,
black against the stars,
waiting for the weather to turn.

Laundry Flaps from Balconies Like Flags

The sounds of car horns,
salsa music,
children in playgrounds,
barking dogs,
and occasional gun shots
rise out of Catia,
one of the largest working-class neighborhoods in South America.

It is a sea of multi-tiered, tin-roofed brick shacks
that cling to the mountains
around Caracas.

Uncollected garbage rots
in the streets
and tangled wires pirating electricity
weave from house to house.

Sporadically rising out of this neighborhood
are dilapidated concrete apartment buildings
with laundry flapping from the balconies like the flags
of neighborhood nations.

Machinery of Stars

New Year's Eve in Havana
is a million stereos bubbling
out of a single electric stew,
flames spurting from the speakers,
windows and tilted bottles of rum.

Apartments burst with people
dancing onto balconies,
spilling into the streets to more parties,
neighbors and roasting pigs.

Children on rooftops fly kites,
hooking ribboned tails into the sky
where the tired white fish of the moon
swims in circles.

Shadows creep into shadows
kissing and drinking
as music thumps over rooftop antennas
and laundry lines.

A family on a porch beats
on overturned buckets
while a man in an orange hat
strums an out-of-tune guitar,
a woman plucks the bass
as the trumpet player's belly
bounces to the beat.

People are falling over,
tipping their cups,
holding onto each other,
laughing over the crumbling sidewalks.

Couples press tight,
dance in the confetti-charged air.

The night is drunk on its own sounds,
heavy with the sulfur smell of fireworks
shooting like flaming Christmas trees
into the machinery of the stars.

The city makes love until the spent,
sweaty husk of afterward,
the pause before the hangover,
the longing to go back.

28

Part III
Streetscapes: Where the Waves Gather

The Street's Empty Stomach

Trees crackle like desire in the sunshine,
an orchestra of kisses
singing the world into a home.

The silent horses of hungry monuments
gallop through their famous cities,
past refrigerated fireworks popping
outside the windshield's wine-bottle view.

Holy credit cards have been put out to pasture.

The map is the last thing keeping our hearts together
as we walk down the street's empty stomach.

Streets Are Straps that Hold the City Down

Streets are straps that hold the city down
when the trains have all gone home
and children mistake skyscrapers for stars.

Buses are run into the ground
with white line burials and asphalt prayers.

Creeping over the horizon,
boats arrive from all over,
names tattooed on their sides
in languages no one understands.

They slush past, homeless packages of world-worn mail,
coated with stamps, floating on,
returning to the sender and back again,
never reaching their mailbox destination.

Signs sprout from everywhere,
telling people where they're going,
where they've been.

Artificial Dawn

Narrow streets are canyons of color
during India's Diwali celebrations.

Blue, gold, and green explosions
dance in the sky.

Rockets shoot out of backyards and rooftops
as terrified dogs bark across the city.

Fireworks hit rickshaws and bicycles
as they pass each other,
bouncing through streets like pinballs
constricted by turns, corners, people, cars.

The streets are a patchwork of colors and pedestrians,
moving like a school of fish.

Pyrotechnics relentlessly pound the air
in crackles and sparks,
charging at speed
out of the sulfur haze.

Echoes of echoes against echoes
push against the dark,
turning the night
into an artificial dawn.

Archives of the Street

History is in the veins of La Paz, Bolivia,
in the archives of the streets,
the stains left by burning barricades,
the bullet holes that scar government buildings.

It marks the city itself.
Indigenous rebel Túpac Katari launched his 1781 siege
against the Spanish from what is now the hilltop K'illi K'illi park.

President Villarroel was hung from a lamp post
by an angry crowd in the Plaza Murillo in 1946.

Another coup rained machine gun fire down the streets of San Pedro in 1979.

Protesters in 2003 pulled train cars from the tracks
and onto a highway during an uprising,
blocking the military from the road
out of the city through the high plains.

A new layer of history marks the city now.

If these plazas had tally marks,
how many coups could be counted?
How many revolutions and counter-revolutions,
failed or otherwise?
How many tyrants, visionaries, and puppets
filled the presidential palace?

The government counts the votes,
the centuries count the dead,
and the people keep on marching
with their banners, checkered rainbow flags, and dynamite.

Streets Sweat Dust

Streets sweat dust.

The dust turns to frozen
mud at night.

New coffins are piled high in the cemetery.

Wealthy bankers at the bar
ask the singer to play
a well-known homage to Che Guevara
while a grandmother asks for change
in front of a Sony store
where the TVs on display
are almost as big as the cars outside.

At midnight, children go through the garbage for dinner,
then kick around a worn out soccer ball
on their way downtown.

Car alarms keep the dogs company.

There is No Wind, Only the Cool Residue of Night

Buildings rise from the market streets of Delhi
like a drunken sculptor threw them there.

The scales of neon ads peel off decrepit walls.

Drums and prayer music sweep across the city,
over rooftops and traffic.

The sidewalks are tired.

Cows parade the road with a regal authority.
They are islands in the organismal city
surrounded by buses and rickshaws.

A low foggy haze clings
to the crude buildings
spread out across the horizon
as birds and monkeys talk
in silent trees.

A train whistle plows through the air,
its slow rush pushing mechanically over the city.

Dogs howl and snap over garbage.

Camels pull carts in the streets
as cars and bicycles rush past hesitatingly.

Holy men mumble prayers and songs
while wading through the city streets.

The road is made up of vehicles and heads,
a river of bobbing buses and cows.

There is no wind,
only the cool residue of night.

Part IV
Riding Through the Wilderness: On the Edges of Maps

Rocking Breathlessly Down

The neon green bus wails its horn,
charging through traffic in the pounding rain.

It's a beast exploding puddles
past dense, fogged forests
that wind down the mountains,
with the descending road
wrapping quickly around sharp turns,
the raging jumble of heavy metal on wheels
rocks breathlessly down.

Inside, packed passengers are soaked by rain
leaking through windows and roof,
as the bus rushes on, unstoppable.

In the shadow of our destination,
a cow silently wades through dirt-dusted streets.

Damp branches of morning are cool.

Bugs buzz at the last dominion of the leaving night.

Street alleys open up to the river
hissing past, cold and steady.

Temples press up against one another along the bank,
seeking warmth.

The relentless water presses on,
unrestrained, unhesitating through mountains,
valleys, villages, in a sacred, sure movement toward the ocean.

Animal Bus

The bus is a hot, rattling creature,
gripping the passengers in a skeleton embrace.

The skin of its tall seats
is a hide of torn plastic where families are crammed
with their goods, bags, and children.

Passengers wave fans of newspapers,
pumping the still air
as a heart does to blood.

The driver hums and slaps
his hands on the cheek of the wheel
to salsa music.

A plastic cross and red curtains
beat valvular time against the windshield,
which proclaims: Only your love.

Gnarled trees and sunburned pastures
twist out of the landscape,
grasping at the hot air
where cows shimmer in the distance.

The air is pregnant with humidity.

Jungle streams spurt
from cliffs
in bursting silver veins.

Empty Grottos on a Jungle Road

An old man hauls a massive marching drum
down the street and through a doorway,
while we gulp down coffee so hot it burns our ears
and crawl into a bus leaving for the jungle.

Steep, steaming mountains shoot up
behind the broken windows and empty chairs
of the rest stop where a lone dog guards a building
flanked by chickens, moss-covered outhouses,
and an outdoor sink blooming with mold.

A local with a shirt riding high
above his glistening belly
walks past a grotto, empty of its virgin Mary
as a pig snores in the road.

Families bathing in the river
slap clothes clean against rocks
to the pulsing perfume
of fried chicken and bus brakes.

Across one crumbling wall
graffiti pleads,
"Youth – do not rise up,
the system is working."

The Jungle's Miniature City of Light

Mist welcomes passengers filing off the bus
at the midnight checkpoint.

Piles of crackers, candy, coca leaves, and soda
glitter in roadside vendors' feeble lights.

Travelers whisper and wander off to piss
while soldiers search for drugs
to the tinny soundtrack of cheers
from a televised soccer match

"We pay better than narco-traffickers,"
read the rusted words on a government sign.

The bus driver whistles sharply,
beeps twice: we are legal, for now.

As we shrug out of the checkpoint's miniature city of light
into the waiting jungle
a voice from the TV blasts,
"Gooooaaaalll!!!"

Motorcycles are Mosquitoes Swarming the Border

In Ciudad del Este, Paraguay
neon Virgin Marys
reach for the streets
teeming with hookahs, sausages, blonde wigs.

"Do you want musical condoms
that play salsa, meringue and tango?"

Piles of huge white lions
printed on heavy blankets
roast in the stifling heat.

"Do you want something bigger?"
one vendor asks, offering up handgun.
"I can get bazookas, machine guns, todo."

Near the bridge to Brazil, a squeaking chorus of packing tape fills the air
where goods are prepared for transport,
and motorcycles hover like carrier mosquitoes
overloaded with boxes and bags,
ready to swarm across the border.

The Horizon's Broken Glass

A man waves from a barbershop
named "Christ is Coming."

Graffiti next door proclaims, "Coca or Death."

A woman walks past with an armload of kittens.

A sticker above the bus driver's head says,
"Better to lose one minute in life
than life in one minute."

We eat in a roadside restaurant
with laundry drying above our heads
and a soap opera playing at full volume.

The mountains on the horizon rise like broken glass,
their shadows advancing with each heartbeat.

Mountains Flare up Like a Fever

A pair of cow heads
are hauled into market
from the back of a muddy station wagon.

Garbage trucks gather their loot.

Wind makes the flags tight.

A man sprints past with a tuba over his shoulders.

Barbershops are so bored they shave themselves.

Christmas lights cover the palm trees.

The seats on the bus sink with our weight.

The air inside smells like strawberry perfume
at the bottom of a swamp.

Moss grows on everything that is not moving.

Slivers of rain fizzle
as they hit the hot ground.

The whole world steams as the sun comes out
and lashes at the mountain peaks,
which flare up like a fever before dark.

Peaks Breathe Clouds

Guests from last night's party wake up shivering
in the grass on the side of the road.

At the airport café
bananas are wrapped in plastic
and cans of Red Bull have a halo of dust.

The flight attendant passes out
ham and cheese sandwiches
cut into the shape of stars.

Scarred mountains below breathe clouds.

When the plane lands,
a Coca-Cola sign welcomes us:
"Smile, you're in Sucre."

A team of women swing pick axes
and push shovels in road construction
next to pigs nosing through garbage.

The main plaza in town is shaded, cool,
smells like dirt and dog urine.

Windows of a car at a stoplight are smeared
with greasy fingerprints.

Pyramids of oranges rise
from blue tarps in front of women in the market.

The bus speakers sing,
"this secret love of ours hurts my heart,
but I'll wait for you."

Part V
Water Worlds: Seas of Possibility

Landlocked Tropical Fish

It is the sunrise on the mountains
outside Santiago, Chile,
the sugar-spiked smile
on the tourist with the strange rash,
the ephemeral, sweaty joy
of political victory.

Naked bodies and the bad teeth of politicians
smile from the covers of magazines,
flapping in the wind on the newsstands
like dried scales on a landlocked tropical fish.

The dogs are pregnant,
the flamingos are plastic,
even the Coca-Cola tastes different.

On the outskirts of town, they sell postcards
of the famous mountains you can never see
through the smog of collective amnesia.

The tourists think it's so cute.
They buy a dozen copies of the same picture,
writing home,
"The waterfalls are lovely
and the pumas are so very real."

Flaming Waterfalls

We are a broken motorboat floating down a river
whose name was bought up by a mining company.

The air is so heavy it might as well be Sunday.

Even the birds are tired.

They swoop drunkenly from branch to branch.

The dogs' breath smells like pickled barks.

A dazed dragonfly flutters through the sun's vague furnace.

Trees reach out for their own shadows.

Jungle eats away at the city.

The waterfalls are so polluted they catch on fire,
their sparks shooting like stars across the land.

Green Violence of the Jungle

Sun and clouds make sure
these mountains are never one color.

Vegetation clings to their powerful sides,
catching light as cliffs thrust upward,
where the green violence of the jungle
meets the inverted sea of the sky.

A massive rock below does not move
in its river of roiling water.

The river bubbles,
wrestles with itself;
a brown fury.

It hugs and rejects the land in each movement,
doesn't care about anything
but its destination: down.

The river's self-conscious brute force
flexes past mountains,
gathering urgency.

Its end is the anticlimax
of a flat lake or ocean,
maybe a drinking glass.

The Dark Sea Laps

Broken circles of cloud
ring the shivering ocean.

Distant lightning at sea ignites the horizon
while fishermen whistle
on white rolling sand.

The melodic hush of the relentless waves
gives and takes from the shore.

Land and water
collide gently on sand
without argument.

In the breath-like fusion of two mysteries,
the dark sea laps.

Clouds shine idly beneath the sun.

Sunset is an oily smear of color against the sky,
its varied hues stretched tight.

Waves with rolling stones sing
as crabs dart to water.

Boats float along walls of trees,
bushes and tangled branches
that sit unmoving
while a passenger train glides past.

At night, the land is darker
than even the starred sky above.

It rests like the fur of a mammal,
with boats, people, animals, birds
crawling in and out of its hairy depths.

Huts dwell and fires crackle.

Wooden fishing nets are lit up
and scoop down
with arms that are spiders' arms
holding nets,
lifting fish out of dark water.

The minute splash of small wooden boats,
then a rooster crows
into the silence
and distant thunder of the sea,
which pushes through humid night air
as boats dip oars and nets.

A Sea of Possibility

Shoreline inhales and exhales
the ocean.

A fisherman handles his invisible lines
like puppet strings,
yanking, pushing, pulling and smoothing
out the air in front of him.

Garbage rides the current,
smashes against the moss-covered rocks on the shore.

A mile away, twin smokestacks puff smoke.

Barges and ships ooze past.

Travel ends and begins at the ocean's horizon,
a sea of possibility.

Another Dictator in the Palace by the River

In the morning in Asunción, Paraguay
the trucks and buses take to the streets
with a vengeance,
making up for the night's lost time.

The smell of fresh bread blends
with the pungent aroma
of burning garbage.

Dogs pace their yards and driveways
behind fences, dreaming and going insane.

Butterflies hover lazily,
bewildered in the exhaust-choked trees.

As the sun bakes the streets,
ancient buses rumble by like urban dragons
trapped in the wrong century.

Years of war,
of successful and unsuccessful coups,
decades of police crackdowns.

Each bullet hole on the downtown light posts tells a story.

The size,
the angle of the ricochet,
all tell of an escape, a death,
another dictator in the palace by the river.

Flash Flood

The sky breaks into hail
falling like a truckload of marbles
on rooftops and windshields.

Rain transforms the streets into rivers
flowing into the sudden lakes of intersections.

People wade knee deep in water
as currents white crest around corners.

Cars plow through the torrent,
roaring engines,
their headlights' dim glow in the muck.

Water laps into living rooms
as people barricade their doors and windows.

A single newspaper stand is set free of its anchor,
and sails down the street's night river.

Cows of the Night

Is it raining or is the town sweating?
Some people are wearing plastic bags on their heads.

A white fluffy poodle with a fresh haircut
smirks from the front seat
next to a woman licking dripping slices of mango.

We pass Lake Titicaca, passengers snore.
The windows fog up.
Hotel California plays on the bus stereo.

Everything begins to look small
because the mountains are so big.

After dark in Sorata
we are greeted by the cows of the night
chewing the grass in the soccer field.

Across the valley,
car headlights move in the mountain forest
like descending submarines.

The red dirt road leads to a cave with paddleboats idling
in an underground lake.

A local tells us the condors attack the cows.
They go for the eyes first.

Burning River

Bicycles zip past,
colliding near temples.

Pigs scrub the streets,
goats gallop,
a cow stands still.

The swarming disjointed mass
of the road slams metal against chrome.

Car horns scream below
a pale moon hanging in the night sky.

Stone steps lead down to the water
from temples.

An old boat floats down the Ganges
with half-burnt body parts from open funeral pyres
bobbing between surfacing dolphins.

Along the water are dark buildings,
castles, temples, mosques,
some looking older than the river itself.

Monkeys on rooftops screech and dance
as people bathe in prayer,
waste deep in water.

In the river's hazy fog,
a lone fish jumps.

Corpses burn in bright
cremation fires,
their sparks rise and fall,
swallowed by the rushing
holy waters.

Part VI
Homeward: The Road is a Hammock for Our Hearts

We All Go Home Like Tears Crying Backwards

Future flashes like the eyes of deer at night
lit up by headlights,
while all across the world
airplanes feast like wonderful lightning.

And we wonder why the skies are so silent.

Their brain is a jagged earring laugh,
hunting, ceaselessly attentive,
foolproof in the autumn light.

We pretend to surrender
like old flowers,
and Uruguay is no goodbye bird.

Our heart becomes a toolshed of resistance,
a universal tent of "I am asleep now."

And then we all go home like tears crying backwards.

A Train Whistle is the Night Writing a Letter to Itself

The deserted street is ill lit,
as quiet as an empty swimming pool.

A neon light flickers at the air,
which is wet
with the night's saliva.

Bugs slap against each other,
against the street lights.

Fog creeps from the bay
into alleyways,
hugging the city.

A group of drunk people laugh
down the far end of one street,
then disappear.

The muffled bark of an indoor dog sounds off.

A television forms a supernatural
tent of light outside one home.

Trees shiver
in their leaves.

A window flutters open
as someone dashes out a bucket of water,
which bounces and scatters
until it is finally digested
by the street itself.

Night is the light left on after the shop is closed,
the train whistle writing a letter to itself
out of loneliness.

Wind in the Supermarket

The hotel room fan turns the sun into a strobe light
and all the flowers are on sale.

It's Valentine's Day in Paraguay
unless it's cancelled by a coup d'etat.

Asunción is a forest of buildings next to a river.

Dengue fever is everywhere,
and so are the mosquitoes and anti-mosquito pesticides.
Men with tanks on their backs pump the poison through the neighborhood.
The mosquitoes keep biting.

On the boat to Uruguay everyone is drinking beer.
We don't spot any sea monsters until we get to the beach.
One with whiskers is washed up on the shore
among the carcasses of a thousand black beetles.

The Uruguayan surfers watch the ocean,
watch the waves,
seeing an invisible rhythm.

The wind blows and blows
through an open door in the supermarket,
making the fruit fresher,
the prices cheaper
and the dust grittier in the suddenly cold air.

The list of destinations at the harbor blinks
on the departure screen until
one of them says 'home.'

What Every Moon Needs

Whatever sound there is
is from the imagination of the moon
sorting numbers,

deciding
on a map
of places
it cannot afford to go.

The moon

is in love with going,
but is as motionless as a birth
in motion,

is a reminder
of the great moments
in other people's lives

attending to darkness
(where watching and moving are)
like a silent
snowstorm
in orbit,

something that wants to leave its own finality

and descend to earth
where its own face can
be on the face of the water
as they both shiver

while the moon grips with its grin and
eats its rippling reflection.

The Road is a Hammock for our Hearts

The city flashes in the neon glow
of a place reborn, killed, and reborn again.

My room slowly fills with dead insects.
Even after you kill the cockroaches, they still move.

Piles of fish are stacked into the backs of trucks,
their stench stewing in the air.

The liquor store is named after a saint
people pray to when they have a hangover.

Houses advance up surrounding hillsides like soldiers,
sending reports back, until, one by one, they claim a new peak.

We wake up to a barbershop silence,
when everywhere smells like cold hamburger
and tastes like lightning.

Trees make the plaza a cave
below a geography of rooftops.

The road is a hammock for our hearts,
a rainstorm that cools the land after a heat wave.

We dance to the dial tone,
leaving messages on midnight's answering machine,
knowing that sometimes what breaks a heart can also fix it,
and nothing buries the dead better than time.

95

Photo Locations

Page 3, Sucre, Bolivia
Page 5, Coroico, Bolivia
Page 7, Uttarakhand, India
Page 9, Miami, Florida
Page 11, Potosí, Bolivia
Page 13, Havana, Cuba
Page 17, Havana, Cuba
Page 19, La Paz, Bolivia
Page 21, El Alto, Bolivia
Page 23, Sucre, Bolivia
Page 25, Havana, Cuba
Pages 27-29, Havana, Cuba
Page 33, Havana, Cuba
Page 35, Havana, Cuba
Page 37, Jodhpur, India
Page 39, El Alto, Bolivia
Page 41, Sucre, Bolivia
Page 43, Delhi, India
Page 47, Uttarakhand, India
Page 49, Copacabana, Bolivia

Page 51, Chapare, Bolivia
Page 53, Cochabamba, Bolivia
Page 55, El Alto, Bolivia
Page 57, El Alto, Bolivia
Page 59, El Alto, Bolivia
Page 61, El Alto, Bolivia
Page 65, Copacabana, Bolivia
Page 67, Lake Titicaca, Bolivia
Page 69, Achocalla, Bolivia
Page 71, Kerala, India
Page 73, Kerala, India
Page 75, Achocalla, Bolivia
Page 77, El Alto, Bolivia
Page 79, La Paz, Bolivia
Pages 81-83, Varanasi, India
Page 87, La Cumbre, Bolivia
Page 89, Sucre, Bolivia
Page 91, Cochabamba, Bolivia
Page 93, El Alto, Bolivia
Page 95, El Alto, Bolivia

Acknowledgements

I am grateful to all of the friends I made in the travels described in this book, from Paris bookstores and train stations in India to protests in Argentina and Havana bars. I would like to give a hug across time and distance to all of the wonderful people I met on the road.

Thanks so much to Marc Estrin and Donna Bister of Fomite Press for believing in this project and making it happen through various drafts. Thanks to my mother, Suzanne Summers, my original editor and reader, for her ongoing enthusiasm for my writing. Thanks to Bill Wroblewski for suggesting the cover photo shot. Thanks also to AK Press, which published earlier work where a few of these pieces of writing also appeared.

I would especially like to thank my wife and travel companion, April Howard. Our journey together began decades ago as we traveled through many of the places described in this book. We experienced our first street barricades in Bolivia together, and shortly after celebrated Valentine's Day in Paraguay. Her own shining enjoyment and command of language has elevated and improved much of the writing I did for this book. I am grateful for her as we continue on the road, now with our sweet and adventurous children, Leon and Eulalia, enriching the journey.

About the Author

Benjamin Dangl has a PhD in Latin American history from McGill University and a BA in writing from Bard College. He is a Lecturer of Journalism and Communication at the University of Vermont. Dangl has worked as a journalist around the world, covering social justice issues, protest movements, and politics for dozens of outlets including T*he Guardian, Vice, The Nation,* and *Al Jazeera.* He is the author of the books *The Price of Fire: Resource Wars and Social Movements in Bolivia, Dancing with Dynamite: Social Movements and States in Latin America,* and *The Five Hundred Year Rebellion: Indigenous Movements and the Decolonization of History in Bolivia,* which won a Nautilus Book Award. He lives in Burlington, Vermont with his family.

Website: BenDangl.com

Fomite

Writing a review on social media sites for readers will help the progress of independent publishing. To submit a review, go to the book page on any of the sites and follow the links for reviews. Books from independent presses rely on reader-to-reader communications.

More poetry from Fomite...

Fomite

For more information, or to order any of our books, visit:

fomitepress.com/our-books.html